D0518195

Houghton Mifflin
Picture
Dictionary

Houghton Mifflin

Picture

Dictionary

Robert L. Hillerich

Illustrations by Maggie Swanson

Houghton Mifflin Company   Boston

Atlanta   Dallas   Geneva, Illinois   Lawrenceville, New Jersey   Palo Alto   Toronto

Cover illustrations, clockwise from top left: **team, bear, dry.**

Copyright © 1986 by Houghton Mifflin Company. All rights reserved. No part of this work may be reproduced or transmitted in any form or by any means, electronic or mechanical, including photocopying and recording, or by any information storage or retrieval system, except as may be expressly permitted by the 1976 Copyright Act or in writing by the Publisher.

All correspondence and inquiries should be addressed to Trade and Reference Division, Houghton Mifflin Company One Beacon Street, Boston, MA 02108

Library of Congress Cataloging-in-Publication Data
Hillerich, Robert L., 1927–
    Houghton Mifflin picture dictionary.
    Summary: A picture dictionary of the vocabulary common in preschool and early school years, presenting for each word a labelled illustration and sometimes a sentence using the word. Includes some cross-references and a section showing how words relate to one another.
    1. Picture dictionaries, English. [1. Picture dictionaries] I. Swanson, Maggie, ill. II. Houghton Mifflin Company. III. Title.
PE1629.H55   1986   423   86-10423
ISBN 0-395-41397-4

Manufactured in the United States of America

Preface

HOUGHTON MIFFLIN PICTURE DICTIONARY
A Note to Teachers and Parents

The dictionary is a basic tool for reading and writing that everybody must learn to use. The *Houghton Mifflin Picture Dictionary* is designed to provide the help and encouragement young children need now, in the preschool and early primary years, as well as to provide the readiness that will be needed in the future for more advanced levels of dictionary use.

Present Needs

In the preschool and early school years, the uses children find for a picture dictionary are different from the uses they will later make of other dictionaries. They use a picture dictionary initially as another picture book: as a source of sheer enjoyment and as a stimulus for expanded thinking to extend the associations they are beginning to make between words and objects, actions, or feelings. Typically in kindergarten and first grade, they also use the picture dictionary as a treasury of ideas, as a source of words they might want to write, and as an aid in reading new words or words that are not yet wholly familiar.

The *Houghton Mifflin Picture Dictionary* has been published to meet these present needs of children. The openness of its design and the quality of its illustrations—all by Maggie Swanson, the distinguished children's illustrator—invite children to enter the book. Because children already "know" most words they will want to look up, words have been carefully chosen from studies of children's reading, speaking, and writing vocabularies. The dictionary word list—including words shown in the brief accompanying workbook, *Vocabulary Building and Dictionary Skills*—was compiled from an analysis of ten different word counts. Among these counts are words common to first-grade reading programs (Barnard and DeGracie 1976), as well as words used by first-graders in speaking (Moe 1982) and writing (Hillerich 1978), and words used in elementary school materi-

als of all kinds (Carroll *et al.* 1971). Not all such words are included in the dictionary because some cannot be illustrated in pictures and sentences that accurately show meaning, and we want the *Houghton Mifflin Picture Dictionary* to provide the kind of information that children can understand. In listening and speaking, children soon come to know a word like *fine*, for instance, meaning "excellent" or "in good health," but during these early years a dictionary cannot teach them its meaning, and lacking meaning, children will be frustrated in finding its spelling.

Even so, this dictionary contains a large proportion of the words they have used and want to write, and words that they have seen or ought to have seen in their reading. Included are many high-frequency words, like *was* or *the*, because these are the words that are most difficult for children to remember in reading or spelling. Nine full- or double-page illustrations at the back of the book—signaled by a colored border around the key word in the dictionary itself—show how words relate to one another. Words in these pages are presented in attractive and familiar settings and are easy to see and read.

Other picture dictionaries often use miscellaneous proper names—Sue and Jim and Alice and Joe—to try to avoid the constant use of pronouns. But such random names have no reality or warmth. In the *Houghton Mifflin Picture Dictionary* there are a number of family groupings whose members appear in illustrations and example sentences. With continuing use of the *Picture Dictionary*, children will come to recognize these people and their pets as familiar friends.

Readiness Skills

A picture dictionary should entertain, but it can do much more through informal learning. First, it can show a child what a "word" is by using entry words.

Second, it can list words in alphabetical order, so that children understand that words in a dictionary are arranged in a sequence and that the sequence is alphabetical. Further, it can help to give the child early experience with the alphabet, in a comfortable setting.

Third, it can acquaint a child with the idea of aids to finding his or her place in a dictionary by including key pictures ("magic pictures") for initial letters. Children are helped to remember the sound each of those letters may stand for when trying to find a word. This unique feature also offers reinforcement for understanding beginning sounds and for letter-sound associations in reading.

Fourth, a picture dictionary can acquaint the child with simple cross references by using entry words that refer to pages at the end of the book. Fifth, it can suggest a sense of the interrelationships among words through the use of those pages and develop a number of other thinking skills, and, sixth, its example sentences serve as story starters.

Helping Children Get Started

Provide children with an overview of the book, so that they can get an idea of what's in it. Point out that many dictionary words are printed in special type in sentences that help children figure out what those words mean. Show some of the full- and double-page illustrations and talk about them. Allow opportunity for browsing and questions.

At another time, tell children about the alphabetical sequence. Show them that all the words beginning with "a" are under the key picture "a," and so on. Show them how the key picture suggests the letter sound.

Later, go through some other letters of the alphabet in the same way. Eventually, pick out one of the dictionary words (like *game*) that is cross referenced to the illustrations at the back of the book and explain the cross-referencing system (the colored border around an entry word means that word, together with related words, can be found in the pages with edges of the same color in the back of the book). Demonstrate and encourage use of the dictionary as a source of ideas for writing and an aid to spelling.

Mainly, however, the role of the teacher or parent should be that of initiator and interested associate. Help your children have fun with language, and success will surely follow.

Robert L. Hillerich

Aa

apple

a • an

A bear is in my room. Why is an old bear there?

add

afraid

Max is afraid of the dog.

able

Max is able to climb.

afternoon

Dan takes a nap in the afternoon.

again

Jill slides. Now she slides again.

air

airplane

airport

all

We are all in the picture.

alphabet

The alphabet starts with **ABC**.

am

I am a boy!

angry

Freddie takes mother's steak. Mother is angry.

and A bear and an owl are in my room.

animal

horse

elephant

wolf

answer

We add 2 and 2. The answer is 4.

answer

Dan can answer the telephone.

apple

are

We are girls!

4

ask

May Ling asks for a pencil.

asleep

The baby is asleep.

ate

Freddie ate all his food.

aunt

Aunt Pat is mother's sister.

Bb

boot

baby

babies

back

Dan has a number on his back.

bad

Freddie is a bad dog.

bag

ball

balloon

banana

bark

The puppy barks at the cat.

bark!

barn

baseball

basket

basketball

bat

I hit the baseball with a bat.

bat

A bat is an animal. It can fly.

bath

We give Freddie a bath.
We get wet.

bear

brown bear

panda

polar bear

teddy bear

8

beat

Can a turtle beat a rabbit in a race? Can the turtle win?

bed

bell

big

Freddie is big. His house is small.

bike

bird

cardinal

wren

blue jay

birthday

On my birthday I am six years old.

bite

Freddie takes a bite of Ching Wah's sandwich.

black

blow

María can blow up a balloon.

blue

board

Grandfather holds a big board.

boat

sailboat

motorboat

ferryboat

book

Animal Stories

bowl

MAX

box

shoe box

boxes

cardboard box

toy box

boy

A boy is a young man.

branch

branches

breath

Ramón can see his breath on the window.

bridge

break Max breaks the cup.

brother

Rob is my brother. We have the same mother and father.

brown

bunch

Here is a bunch of flowers.

bunches

building

house   apartment building   house   school

bunny

bunnies

bus

buses

button

burn

The wood burns.

Ben can button his coat.

Cc

cat

cake

calendar

JULY

S	M	T	W	T	F	S
				1	2	3
4	5	6	7	8	9	10
11	12	13	14	15	16	17
18	19	20	21	22	23	24
25	26	27	28	29	30	31

call

Ben can call grandmother.

camera

camp

can

Here is a can.

candy

candies

can

Aunt Pat says, "Yes, you can walk."

cannot

Aunt Pat says, "No, you cannot walk."

cap

car

card

carrot

cartoon

A cartoon tells a story with pictures.

cat

catch

Freddie likes to catch the ball.

catcher

chicken

chief

Mr. Deer Fox is a chief.

CHIEF DEER FOX

chair

straight-back chair

rocking chair

armchair

child

A child is a young person.

children

church

churches

circle

circus • circuses

city • cities

classroom

clean

Freddie had a bath, and now Freddie is clean.

climb

Aunt Pat can climb the ladder.

clock

digital

cuckoo

desk

alarm

clothes

A shirt and coat are clothes.

coat

cold

Ice is cold. Jill is cold.

brrrr!

club

The children have a club.
They plant trees together.

color

See the colors.

color

We color the pictures.

computer

cone

cook

Dad likes to cook.

cookie

cool

Jill blows on her apple to make it cool.

corn

count

Count the cubes. How many are there?

country

Our house is in the country.

cover

Jill takes the cover off the jar.

cow

cube

cream

Father puts cream on his bananas.

cry

cup

mug

tea cup

mug

cut

24

Dd

duck

dad • daddy

Fran calls her father dad. Dan and Ben call their father daddy.

daisy • daisies

dance

dark

It is dark, and Jill cannot see.

day Morning, afternoon, and night make one day.

dear

Annie starts a letter with "Dear Jack."

deer

Five deer are here.

desk

dictionary

dictionaries

did

Did Ben eat an orange?

dig

different

Alex and Buster are the same. Freddie is different.

dinner

dinosaur

do

How many pencils do you have?

doctor

does

Does Jill have four pencils?

dog

collie

mixed breed

beagle

terrier

28

doll

baby

rag

china

draw

dream

Annie has a dream.

dollar

door

cupboard door

entrance door

screen door

dress

dresses

dress

In the morning, we dress.

drink

Max can drink milk. Amy can drink milk too.

drive

drop

Here is a drop of water.

drop

Watch Fran drop her books.

drum

Ben has a drum.

dry

They dry Freddie.

duck

E e

e

egg

ear

elephant

child

rabbit

earth

Here is the earth.

earth

Plants grow in the earth.

east

The sun rises in the east.

easy

Is it easy to ride a bike? It is easy for May Ling.

eat

Watch Freddie eat our dinner.

egg

eight

8

end

The end

equal

Two and two equals four.

evening

The sun sets in the evening.

everybody

Everybody laughs.

eyes

Ff

feather

face
Sara has paint on her face.

fairy • fairies

fall
See Humpty Dumpty fall off the wall.

fall

family

families

farm

fast

The train goes fast.

fat

Here is a fat cat.

father

I call my father dad.

feed

Watch Rob feed the duck.

fence

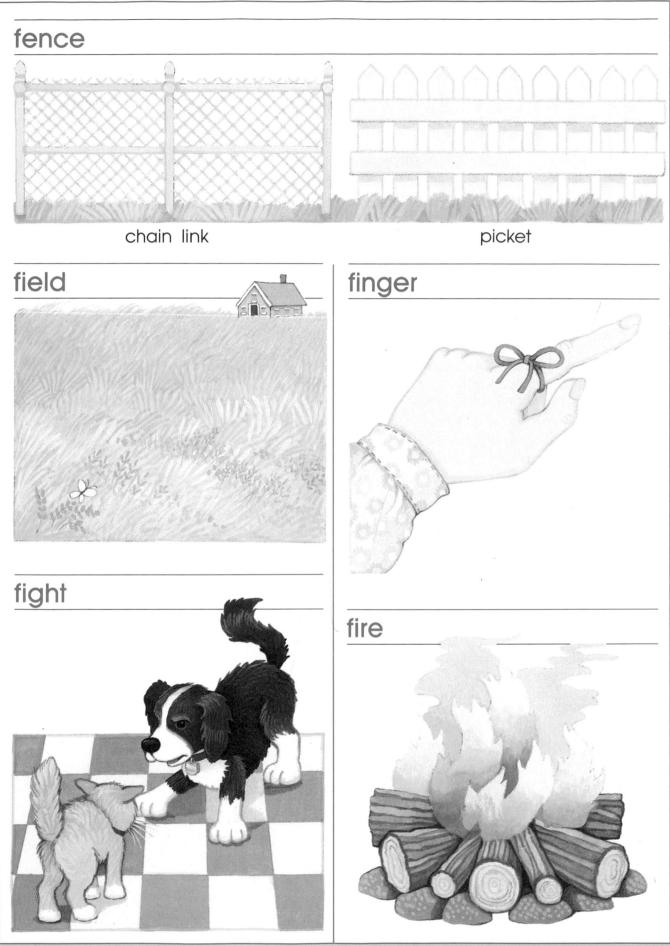

chain link

picket

field

finger

fight

fire

first Fran is first in line.

first grade

fish • fishes

five

flat

floor

flower

The flower is red.

fly • flies

Flies are in the air.

fly

A plane can fly.

fly

May Ling hits a fly

food

foot

feet

football

forest

forget

Did Ben forget his **ABC's**?

A...B...C...

four

friend

fox

foxes

frog

free

funny

María gets a free kitten.

Gg

ghost

game

garden

get

I get a book.

ghost

giant

42

girl

A girl is a young woman.

give

Give Ben a book.

glass

glasses

glasses

glue

go The cars go.

goes One car goes.

gold

goose

geese

grandfather

We call our grandfather grandpa.

grandmother

We call our grandmother grandma.

grass

green

grow

We see Fran grow.

guess

Hh

h

hat

had

Dan had an apple and a pear.

hair

half

Here is half for you. Here is half for me.

Halloween

hand

hang

happy

hard

It is hard to ride a bike up the hill.

hard

The walk is hard.

has

Dan has an apple and a pear.

hat

police

top

firefighter

baseball

have

Dan and Ben have apples and pears.

head

One turtle has his head out. One turtle has his head in.

he

He is Sam.

heart

her

Her sweater is blue.

here

Write your name here.

high

The balloon is high in the sky.

hill

hide

his

His sweater is green.

hit

Ben can hit the ball.

hold

María holds the cup.

hole

home

Home is the place where we live.

horse

hospital

hot

The sun is hot. Jill is hot.

hour

An hour is part of a day.

house

how many

How many raccoons do you see? I see six!

hundred

100

hungry

Freddie is hungry.

hunt

Father hunts for his keys.

hurt

Max hurt his leg.

Ii

igloo

I

I am Dan.

ice

I skate on the ice.

is

He is Rob. She is Fran.

it

It is a kitten.

Jj

jack-in-the-box

jar

Here is the jar.

jet

juice

I like juice.

jump

Ben can jump.

Kk

k

kite

kick

king

kindergarten

kiss • kisses

María gives mother a kiss.

kitchen

kite

The kite goes high.

kitten

knock

Watch Ben knock.

Ll

lamp

ladder

lake

A lake is bigger than a pond.

lady • ladies

57

land

The people see land.

land

Watch the plane land.

large

Large is big.

laugh

leaf

leaves

leave

Watch grandmother leave.
She goes in a car.

58

left

Here is Ben's left hand.

leg

letter

The first letter is **A**.

letter

Mother writes a letter.

lick

lie

We lie on the sand.

light

The sun gives us light.

like

Does Ben like apples?

like

Alex is like Buster. They are the same.

line

Amy draws a line.

line

We stand in a line.

list

little

Dan has a little apple.

live

We live at home.

long

The balloon is long.

lot

A lot of kittens are in the box. Many kittens are there.

low

The swing is too low.

lunch • lunches

Mm m

monster

mail

man

men

make We make a house.

many

Many kittens are a lot of kittens.

map

mark

Mother makes a mark.

mark

Ramón gets his mark. It is an A.

me

They give me a prize.

meat

meet

milk

minute

Ching Wah can eat a carrot in a minute.

mom • mommy

Fran calls her mother mom. Dan and Ben call their mother mommy.

money

monster

moon

morning

Morning is the start of the day.

mother

I call my mother mom.

mountain

mouse

mice

mouth

move

The men move things.

music

They make music.

my

Here is my bed.

Nn

nest

name

Ramón   Jill

nap

nest

new

The brown shoe is new.
The black shoe is old.

night

Night is the end of the
day.

nine

no

Jill says, "No!"

no

She has no bananas
today.

nobody

Nobody is here.

noise

north

The north wind is cold.

not

Freddie does not go.

nothing

Nothing is in the jar.

now

Jump in the pool NOW!

number

octopus

o'clock

It is nine o'clock.

old

The black shoe is old. The brown shoe is new.

one

open

Open the door.

or

Do you like apples or oranges?

orange

It is an orange.

orange

The color is orange.

our

Our dog is Freddie.

owl

P p

pig

page

The book has pages.

paint

pair

A pair is two of the same thing.

pair of socks

pair of mittens

pair of shoes

paper

park

part   The wheel is a part of the bike.

party • parties

pass
The cars pass the truck.

patrol

pay

peach

peaches

pear

pen

pencil

person

people

pet

The kitten is my pet.

pick

Rob can pick the apple.

picnic A raccoon goes to the picnic!

picture

piece

pie

pig

pin

pitcher

May Ling is the pitcher.

place

Jill has a place in line.

plane

plant

It is a plant.

plant

We plant a tree.

play　We give a play.

play

We play with our friends.

please

Please tie my shoes.

point

The pencil has a sharp point.

point

Does May Ling point to the skates?

police

pond

A pond is smaller than a lake.

pony

ponies

pool

potato

potatoes

present

problem

2+2=4

pull

Pull Freddie.

prize   Freddie gets the prize.

pumpkin

puppy

puppies

purple

push

Push Freddie.

put

Put the book on the table.

Qq

quarter

queen

question

Jill has a question.

R r

rabbit

rabbit

A rabbit is a bunny.

raccoon

rain

race

reach

read

Now I read the book.

ready

Ching Wah is ready for school.

red

remember

Did Ben remember his **ABC**'s?

A, B, C, D, E, F, G, H, I, J...

rest

We rest after lunch.

ride

right

Here is Fran's right hand.

right

Annie is right!

right!

ring

Does the telephone ring?

ring

Sara has a ring.

rise

Watch the balloon rise.

robin

river

robot

road

rock

rocket

room

Here is Rob's room.

roll

I eat the roll.

rope

roll   Watch the tire roll.

rose

round

The wheel is round.

row

Row and line are the same.

row

Watch Fran row.

rug

run

Ss

sock

sail

The sail makes the boat go. We sail the boat.

salad

same

Alex and Buster are the same.

89

sand

sandwich

sandwiches

saw

The saw cuts wood.

saw

Watch Cassie saw wood.

save

Watch Fran save her money.

say

Say the **ABC's**.

K-L-M-N-O-P-Q-R...

school

PINE STREET SCHOOL

sea

seat

second

Annie is second in line.

see

See the boat!

seed

sell

We sell juice.

sentence

set

See the sun set.

send

We send a present.

set

Otto has a set of tools.

seven

7

sharp

Cassie has a sharp saw.

she

She is Sara.

sheep

Here is one sheep.

sheep

Five sheep are here.

ship

shirt

shoe

shop

Here is a shop.

shop

We shop in the store.

shore

short

Freddie's friend is short.

show

We watch the show.

show

Show me your new watch.

shut

Shut the door.

sick

side

One side of the paper is white. One side is red.

sign

FREE KITTENS

since

May Ling has been waiting since yesterday to swim.

sing

sister

She is my sister. We have the same mother and father.

sit

We sit.

six

6

skate

María likes to skate.

sled

sleep

Ben and Freddie sleep.

skate

Here is a skate.

sky

slide

small

Dan has the small apple.

smell

The dog can smell a cat.

snow

soap

sock

soft

Too soft!

some

Dan has some balloons.

song

Annie sings the ABC song.

A B C D
E F G
H I J K

sound

soup

south

The birds fly south.

space

The rockets fly in space.

space

Here is the space for a book.

spell

Spell R-o-b.

spring

square

squirrel

stand

star

start

Cassie starts to cut the grass.

station

stay

Freddie has to stay.

step

The first step is red.

step

The baby takes a step.

stick

Glue makes things stick.

stick

Here is a stick.

stone

stop

STOP

store

CLOTHES

storm

story

stories

strong

Dad is strong.

summer

street

sun

supermarket

surprise

What a surprise!

sweater

Her sweater is blue.

swim

Jill can swim.

swing

María is on a swing.

swing

We swing!

T t

tiger

table

tail

dog tail

kite tail

take

Take **an apple.**

talk

Annie and Fran talk.

tall

He is tall.

teach

teacher

Here is the teacher.

team

telephone

television

tell

Watch Ben tell Rob a story.

temple

ten

10

thank

Fran can thank Rob and María.

thank you!

Thanksgiving

the

The old brown bear is in my room.

their

Freddie is their dog.

them

Look at them swim!

there

Jill stands there.

they

They hold Freddie.

thing

Here are five things.

third

Ben is third in line.

three

3

throw

tie

Otto has a red tie.

tie

Mary Jo can tie her shoe.

time

time out!

tire

today

Today is July 8.

together

We are all together.

tomorrow

Tomorrow is July 9.

too

Freddie goes, too.

too

Freddie is too big.

toy

teddy bear

blocks

robot

train

The train goes fast.

tool

You can make things with a tool.

hammer

saw

drill

town

TOYS

BOOK

tree

triangle

trip

They go on a trip.

trouble

Max is in trouble.

truck

dump truck

pickup truck

fire truck

try

See Rob try to win.

turn

It is Annie's turn!

turn

Amy can turn the bike.

turtle

two

2

Uu

u umbrella

umbrella

upstairs

Freddie is upstairs.

uncle

Uncle Jay is dad's brother.

us

Do you have pencils for us?

V v

vest

van

vegetable

celery

carrots

lettuce

corn

very

Here is a very long dog.

visit

Grandfather and grandmother visit us.

Ww

worm

wait

We wait for the bus.

BUS STOP

walk

wall

house wall

stone wall

warm

The house is warm. Dan is warm.

was

Ching Wah was the pitcher.

wash

watch

watches

watch

Watch the game.

water

way

They see the way to the zoo.

we

We swing!

week

Seven days make one week.

SUNDAY	MONDAY	TUESDAY	WEDNESDAY	THURSDAY	FRIDAY	SATURDAY
1	2	3	4	5	6	7

west

The sun goes down in the west.

wet

what

What does Freddie do? He goes to his dinner.

FREDDIE

wheel

bicycle wheel

steering wheel

where

Where is Max?

white

why

Why is Freddie wet?

win

Watch Annie win.

who Who hides from Ching Wah?

wind   The **wind** blows.

wind

Jill can **wind** the toy.

winter

window

woman

women

won

Annie won.

wood

word

world

write

Ben can write.

wrong

Sam is wrong!

wrote

Ben wrote his name.

Xx

x-ray

x-ray

chest   hand

xylophone   The xylophone makes music.

Yy

y

yo-yo

yard

year

May Ling is six years old.

yellow

yes

Yes, she has bananas today.

yesterday

Yesterday was July 7.

you

I am Fran. You are Dan.

young

A young cat is a kitten.

A young dog is a puppy.

A young person is a child.

your

Here is your toy.

Zz

zipper

zebra

zipper

zoo

zero   Zero is the number for nothing.

Astronaut

Skylab

solar panel

Apollo spacecraft

space station

rocket

solar panel

Space Telescope

Saturn V

astronaut

satellite

mechanical arm

cargo bay

rocket engine

tether

space shuttle

helmet

space suit

Body

Doctor's Office

head

hair

eye

nose

teeth

lips

chin

ear

cheek

mouth

neck

shoulder

chest

stomach

waist

wrist

palm

thumb

knee

leg

foot

sole

arm

elbow

hip

hand

finger

thigh

calf

ankle

heel

toe

Classroom

bulletin board

aquarium

fish

calendar

handbells

drum

watering can

tape player

drumsticks

piano

songbook

sink

brushes

scissors

construction paper

triangle

toy truck

paint

blocks

toy car

easel

toy plane

window

chalkboard

gerbil
cage

plant

1 2 3 4

eraser

clock

map

chalk

globe

teacher

computer

table

chair

RICK

maggie

sue

aide

cubbies

Reading Group
book

129

Dinosaur

pterosaur

tyrannosaurus

apatosaurus

triceratops

brachiosaurus

stegosaurus

protoceratops

ornitholestes

Farm

Games and Fun

bat

baseball

jeans

glove

shorts

hopscotch

seesaw

tricycle

hide-and-seek

sled

toboggan

snow woman

igloo

snowman

132

kite

swing

slide

bike

jump rope

pad

shirt

roller skate

hood

snowshoe

ski

snow bird

ear muffs

hockey

puck

mitten

scarf

ice skate

Supermarket

Fruits and Vegetables

tomatoes lettuce beans carrots

scale

fish chicken meat

corn

soap

paper towels

dog food

cat food

pears

potatoes

nuts

peaches

cantaloupes

raisins

lemons

peanut butter

basket

shopping cart

limes grapes

oranges bananas apples

door

milk butter cheese eggs yogurt

frozen fish

cereal

crackers

breads

juices

register

counter

cashier

check out

scanner

macaroni

paper bag

bagger

135

Word

over

under

above

on

off

across

below

behind

below

out

out

in

Zoo

rhinoceros

zebra

polar bear

elephant

giraffe

hippopotamus

seal

lion

cub

camera

balloon

camel

baby stroller

koala

tiger

kangaroo